D1736527

Turning a Train of Thought Upside Down

An Anthology

of Women's Poetry

Edited by Andrena Zawinski

Scarlet Tanager
BOOKS

Copyright © 2012 by Andrena Zawinski
All rights reserved.
Printed in the United States of America.

Cover painting: Michel Demetria Tsouris
Cover and interior design: Marianne Betterly

A special thanks to the following people for their editorial assistance:
Trena Machado, Gloria Rodriguez, and Judy Wells.

Published by Scarlet Tanager Books
P.O. Box 20906
Oakland, CA 94620
www.scarlettanager.com

Library of Congress Cataloging-in-Publication Data

Turning a train of thought upside down : an anthology of women's poetry / edited by Andrena Zawinski.
p. cm.
ISBN 978-0-9768676-2-3 (alk. paper)
1. American poetry--Women authors. 2. American poetry--California--San Francisco Bay Area. 3. American poetry--21st century. I. Zawinski, Andrena.
PS589.T87 2012
811'.60809287--dc23

2011037304

Turning a Train of Thought
Upside Down

Contents

IV ...knowing there must be somewhere to go...

V ...we are beginning to understand something...

VI ...I see the purpose of everything around me...

Preface

After a long day of sending work out to several publications, after negotiating reading dates, after trying to generate new poems and revise older ones, I felt what many writers feel—exhausted and isolated. I found myself wondering what I needed, what any woman might need, beyond the hard work and uncertainty of having my poetry read and heard.

I realized that I missed something deep in my core, that I wanted more than elbow brushing at events or fleeting commentaries on my work, that I wanted to be part of a community of writers beyond traditional exercise or feedback workshops. So, I decided to invite about twenty women to my home one Saturday afternoon for a potluck of poetry and food. They all showed up, and each loved the idea of a social extension of our hard work in poetry, something informal with no membership requirements or deadlines, something that could inspire and rejuvenate. That was in 2007.

As we continued to host Salons at each other's homes—feeding ourselves with food and words with as many as twenty of our more than forty members attending any given Salon—I became more and more excited about the wealth of talent and richness of poetry that we were sharing. Some had begun to form projects outside the group like online and face-to-face workshops or public Salon readings, so the production of an anthology seemed a natural next step for the diversity of writing from these poets, who range from those who have authored several books to those who publish individual poems from time to time.

Poet Lucille Lang Day, one of the original Salon members, responded enthusiastically to the idea of the anthology, finding it to be a perfect project for her press, Scarlet Tanager Books. Since ScarletTanager features the work of West Coast writers, she felt the anthology would complement the press's line of books by individual authors.

The Salon includes journalists, social activists, college professors, doctors, gardeners, lawyers, artists, educators, and women in many other professions. Many members say they find it invaluable to be in a milieu of encouragement and appreciation of each other's writing, along with the unconditional support in a nurturing community of women writers. *Turning a Train of Thought Upside Down*, which is what we often do in the effort to inspire and create poetry, is an expression of the collective voice of the San Francisco Bay Area Women's Poetry Salon. We hope, in the words of Anne Sexton, you will as you read these pages "put your ear down close to your soul and listen hard."

Andrena Zawinski
Alameda, California
January 2012

I

...I'm a gesture of a gesture...

Nellie Hill

Fata Morgana

Sometimes when the shadow of the shadow
knocks on my door and night
walks in speckled and luminescent
with its sea of fireflies flecking the sultry air,
sometimes it remains like that:
a shadowy dream, muted, perfumed.

Then I want to leave through the door
and fling myself at summer gardens.
Then I'm a gesture of a gesture,
all arms, my speech soundless,
almost dream, almost life
and music comes through my window,
enters my eyes, my ears,
and follows me out like a shawl,
hugging my shoulders.

Jeanne Wagner

My mother was like the bees

because she needed a lavish taste
on her tongue,
a daily tipple of amber and gold
to waft her into the sky,
a soluble heat trickling down her throat.
Who could blame her
for starting out each morning
with a swig of something furious
in her belly, for days
when she dressed in flashy lamé
leggings like a starlet,
for wriggling and dancing a little madly,
her crazy reels and her rumbas,
for coming home wobbly
with a flicker of clover's inflorescence
still clinging to her clothes,
enough to light the darkness
of a pitch-black hive

Eileen Malone

How She Brushed Her Hair

I would watch her, sit on the edge of her bed
the reflection of my barefoot boy self
out of range in her dressing table mirror
watch my beautiful mother brush her blackly
beautiful hair, the kind of hair that begs to be
taken out dancing and when I think of dancing
I think of her step light ankled like wild Sika deer

I remember how she brushed her hair
up from the mystery that was herself
catching it, twisting it into a Celtic knot
singing with blackbird voice
her throat whiter than any lily wet with sun
but that was then, and this is now
before she stopped singing, dancing
banished me from sitting on that same bed
she took to, refused to rise from
let the tangles wither in her hair
tossed in fever and deliriums and began to die
and die and die and die and all I want to do
is write about her hair, her hair, the kind of black hair
found only on young Irish women, straight, silken
in its awful glamour of black, how I would sing
into the harp of it silvered with sheen and how
she would sing back, kiss me to sleep
her midnight black hair a halo of incessant scent
of daffodil breath, tea leaves, lily of the valley

sometimes when the boy becomes the man
we have to change the truth in order to remember
someone the way we want to
—I turn the mirror to the wall.

Lynne Knight

What a Shame

When my mother began to lose her mind, shame
stood at the door like a beggar or prince;
she couldn't distinguish. She knew only *Hide*.
So she hid, turning her face into a mask,
shoving her hearing aid into a sock shoved
far back in a drawer, burying her leg brace
under fallen skirts in her overcrowded closet.
Those thieves, she said from behind the mask
while I searched for the hearing aid, brace.

Then disdain fled with the crows she'd seen
on the counter when she went to make her lunch.
You don't make your own lunch, I would say. *You go*
to the dining room. She sat: scared rabbit mask, now.
Don't let it hurt me! her shallow breath pleaded
though she made no sound approaching words.

I pretended none of this was happening to her.
To me. Then one day I came to visit and opened
the door to the stink of shit. In the night
she'd had an attack of diarrhea but couldn't find
the bathroom. She'd run everywhere, hunting.

It's all right, I said after cleaning the mess,
bathing her. *It's all right.* I was tying her
shoes, kneeling before her. She leaned close.
In the two or three seconds she was herself again,
she whispered, *Liar*. And I saw what I owed her.
Shame, whether beggar or prince, had no claim
to her door. What was happening to her could be
happening to anyone. And was. And is.

Rebecca Foust

Mom's Canoe

Do you remember your old canoe?
Wooden wide-bellied, tapered ends
made to slip through tight river bends
swiftly, like shadow.
Hull ribbed delicately, wing of bird
sometimes seen, never heard when it flew
through the water more glider than boat,
ponderous in portage, weightless afloat.
Frail origami, vessel of air,
wide shallow saucer suspended where
shallows met shadows near the old dam.
Remember how it glowed like honey in summer
rubbed with beeswax and turpentine
against leaks, cracks, weather and time.
All your housekeeping went into that canoe,
then you rode high, bow lifted,
arced up like flight, all magic, power,
evening light. You j-stroking,
side-slipping, eddying out, frugal
with movement, all without effort,
just like you walked and ran.
I still see you rising from water to sky,
paddle held high,
river drops limning its edge.
Brown diamonds catch the light as you lift, then dip.
Parting the current, you slip
silently through the evening shadows.
You, birdsong, watersong, slanting light,
following river bend, swallowed from sight.

Ruby Bernstein

Ritual

The house is quiet tonight,
everyone is ready, the waiting begins.
Mother lights the blue candles
perched in the sterling candlesticks.
Her head covered, in Hebrew she recites
the blessing her mother, Rebecca—Rifka—
my namesake, taught her decades ago;
I wait, squirming and shifting from foot to foot,
inhaling the magic of my mother's chicken
slowly simmering in the cast iron pot,
wafting smells of tomatoes and onions—
the *gedempte* chicken, the chicken
of immigrant women.

My mother, tired, has rushed home from work,
rituals to perform before the sun sets over our valley.
On this and every Friday night, she removes
her apron, my father shaves and wears
his best tie; I wash my face and brush
my long, dark curls. Our white pottery plates
standing ready, the chicken calls.

Now on foreign shores—Tashkent, Vilnius, Cairo,
Dushanbe, Qom—lands where I have traveled,
where other mothers pray, I eat alone
on Friday nights, deaf to synagogues' songs,
while memories simmer.

Laurel Benjamin

Fish

The steps and stages in using the seeds of eggplant almost
disappearing, then between, you hear the
mutilated architecture of arousal—
Moorish slopes, Spain of the 1400s, a man sitting in
underground robes, genitals converted

pastries enclosing a forbidden filling.
Forty-nine days
between Shavuot and Passover,
a recipe for cattle in summer pastures, and fish—

boquerón, lubina, bacalao, merluza—

The king would not take silver, amassed for
generations, into honeycombs of the Alhambra—
that would not save the man—
lost among waterwheels
were his keys

departing with the morning light, divine
eggplants and garlic sitting on the window
left to cool, left with
the making of braids, the shelling of pistachios—

The route fanning to a Slavic Empire occurred
without estate or seeming damage
jewels stuffed in a cap. He walked in the stream bed
rather than the sequence of capture and
throat. Not a woman's necklace, but rope assigning outburst,
traditional narrative, chant of the infant in a man—

lenguado, trucha, atún—

Empty space of stream divided the future—
which woman would he marry, would the two-toned woman
become his Christian wife?
They met in the hiding place, less than a room with hay above
waiting for dogs and flashlights, vision of the world
through the unmoving.

Carol Dorf

Fruit of Stories

Demeter and her daughter Persephone:
every woman tells this story with her mother.
Temptation of the thin-skinned juice-filled seeds,
and following that God back to Hades,
wrapping arms around his leathery waist,
as the motorcycle shoots through time and space.

We return to mother with our children,
but she puts the plates of soup in front of them,
while we peel fruit and rinse scummy glasses.
We say, "I didn't know it would be like this,"
and she smiles, folds a towel, and starts humming
a lullaby we could remember if only she'd been patient.

Our daughters won't stop growing; our laps grow
crowded with these half-woman girls. They say, "No!"
when they see breasts softening their bony ribs.
We reply, "It can't be helped." We'd like to stop
feeding them hard-boiled eggs, but they've developed
a taste for that mix of rubber and mush.

We can't close the door or hold back the day
they cut a pomegranate off the tree,
and run through the fields in search of a God.

Bonnie Kwong

Common Flower
for Dorothy

You try to teach me the flowering
order of your garden in spring:
snowdrops, hyacinths, daffodils, tulips...
no, hyacinths, tulips, daffodils, snowdrops...
a forgotten rosary.
You would have me send down
your grandson's roots
in newly thawed Northeastern soil.

In the silence between us, a common flower
grows, a red hibiscus leeward from your house,
a transplant: flower of Caribbean winds
bearing word of your half-sisters,
flower of my childhood strolls
in the mushroomed woods of Asia.
Flower of blood. Nomadic, animal flower.

I note the growing caesuras
between your breaths, your paling skin.

In the silence after you, your grandson and I
will make love in yet another country.
We will see a man feed hibiscus
to an iguana among Mayan ruins.
Scarlet, vegetable flower.

Our daughter will come to us
on the wild tongues of the Pacific,
the coast of your birth.

In a world where flowers travel,
it is impossible to be strangers.

Gail Rudd Entrekin

Deciding

Suppose a mother whose children are gone,
looking at the long straight road ahead,
feeling herself invisible and beside the point,
were to step off into the woods, leave a note
that said *I don't want to live without passion*;
could she erase herself? Could she keep blind
to the holes her betrayal would leave
in all the little boats, the way they would sink
slowly over the long years ahead, those boats
she'd made and set afloat in hope?

Suppose
the woman arrives at the water and finds there
the man she has almost forgotten, waiting for her
in a kayak with red paddles.

And now she gets into
the front and begins to stroke, and they pull together
in silence, dipping and turning, dipping and turning,
two figure eights in the late air. Each time she raises
her paddle, the cool water trickling down along its stem
drops in shiny glints on her bare legs.

And he,
without speaking, matches her stroke, controls
the rudder with his feet, steers them out
onto the glittering green lake, where they see
the sun drop behind the tree line, where they see
eleven ducks in a V beyond the trees
in the grey pall of a fire far away
in someone else's wood,

and the note
she thought of writing becomes
an unremembered dream,
and one lone brown straggler,
flying up from the lake beside them,
calls its desperate wait, wait
as it lifts across the sky.

Judith S. Offer

And Theirs, Them

We are the women of small histories/
    diaries, journals, letters to our sisters/
whose mothers recited earlier accounts
while mixing turkey stuffing or brownies
in any coffee-flavored kitchen.

We are the keepers of lesser treasures/
    relish recipes, songs our uncles sang,
    steps to the old dances/
whose children are relentlessly photographed
and ride the years from sharp to fading
in masks of cellophane.

We are the bearers of background memories/
    his last words, her first song,
    Thanksgiving before the war/
whose grandchildren will grow
to remember us
and theirs, them.

II

...leaping out of the tiny netted strands...

Janell Moon

Descent

We were tethered to each other falling to a deep descent
with only the fragile web to catch us. The net only caused
us to slow down, more hesitant as a family who woke up
struck blind before the day gave out its lie. My brother fell
the farthest. My mother fell wearing her many hands and
dad had on his old slippers. He carried my sister on his back.
She gazed up at the sunny sky. I was next to my brother
who had the finest skin and freshest organs, the one most
desired by midnight monsters who suckled on flailing children.
I tried to catch him. Oh, how my fingers strained to hold onto
the fragile net and the disappearing foot of the boy. I wished
I had stronger legs and could swing us back to the suburban
whirring of lawn mowers. But no, my pounding heart saved
only me by leaping out of the tiny netted strands.

Bonnie Kwong

To Unborn Sons

What languages have you heard
straining through your mothers' tongues
into your surrounding waters?

Mine is a vocabulary of greetings,
souvenirs from times of mock peace:

guten tag   *zo sun*   *namaste*
mata ashita   *hasta mañana*
shalom   *salaam*

Teach me how to say *sorry* in Arabic,
Pashto and Farsi, and I will teach
the son astir in my belly.

In your negative age, counting to zero,
speak to one another in the language
of the unborn, the language of water.
Tomorrow, a different light will fall.

Who among you will befriend another
in a land not your own?
Who among you will negotiate
in a currency not your own?
Who among you will live to tell?
Which language will you choose?

Will you recall the syncopation
in your pregnant mother's pulse—
heartsick premonition—
before composing herself to carry on?

Susan Cohen

Chamber Music

To learn a piece of music
you must get it in your hands.

I was scrambling on my elbows
up the bed, frantic
to back out of maternity.

I see your baby,
the nurse shouted.
Touch its head!

She had to yell until I heard
above the pain.

O, then I reached down
and met his threads of hair,
hot and yolky.

O, then I learned the hard
crescendo of his skull.

Rebecca Foust

Apologies to My Ob-Gyn

Sorry that my boy birthed himself
too early, took up so much room
in your prenatal nursery
with his two pounds, two ounces
and did not oblige your nurses
with easy veins.

Sorry we were such pains in your ass
asking you to answer our night calls like that,
and that he did everything so backwards:
lost weight, gained fluid
blew up like a human balloon
then shriveled.

Sorry about how he defied your prognoses,
skyrocketed premiums, weighted the costs
in your cost-benefit analyses,
skewed bell-curve predictions
into one long, straight line;
sorry he took so much of your time

being so determined to live. He spent
today saving hopeless-case nymph moths
trapped in the porchlight, one matrix-dot
at a time, and now he's asleep; blue wingbeat
pulse fluttering his left temple—there,
there again. Just like it did then.

Barbara Joan Tiger Bass

like water from Angel Falls

after he died
that first week
I called my black clothes
shiva wear

something funny
about distance or a diversion
amidst the flowers
seemed natural

then long days took hold
everywhere places we'd been
before all once
was once again

while joy crept in
sage living room
gold entry playful
sounds ricocheted

my son turned
boyhood into beauty
sputtered random power
curled delicate fists

leaps of faith rounded
into dance on the carpet
turn after turn until
each completion echoed

but nothing led me back
to death
this wash of tears, expected
where final became clear

Dawn McGuire

True North

My son wants True North.
I show him the North
Star. See, I tell him,

Right here, at the tip of the Earth's
axis. It is always in one place.
The whole sky turns around it.

He shakes his head. Polaris
is at least a thousand miles
from the Magnetic North

he tells me. North
should be all in one place.
Isn't that what True means?

Under the night sky
I hear a creature's teeth
debride my son's ninth August.

The dogs pace protectively
around a boy who imagines he can be
All One Thing.

I sometimes tell him
things beyond his years,
like:

if you can protect
the foolishness of one you love,
you will never be without a Friend.

But it will be awhile before I tell him
about magnetic storms;
the fragmenting dislocations

atmospheres force on light;
how everything bends to matter,
breaks; how this

becomes acceptable.
We trace the Big Dipper,
my hand over his.

The handle glints,
the great bowl's spangles
fall toward our home.

Under our fingertips,
Polaris. And this boy
already too big to lift

I lift. A little of the light
that left the double stars
before he was conceived

enters him. When it is time,
though it will tear the last gristle
of the cord from him to me,

cord of my last paradise,
I will face him East.
I will tell him all of this as well.

Lenore Weiss

The Widow Revisits Golfball Graveyard in Dimond Park

Afternoons we stayed in Dimond Park
and mornings, too, when young bodies
sang with new notes inside a pendulum
swinging up and down.

The children climbed monkey bars
and screamed on the slide in the sandbox
where every kind of dog buried its shit
and walked away pleased

until it was time to hike the canyon
filled with mudrocks and ferns.
Green parasols shaded wet feet
as we heaped mouths with blackberries,

and wove fingers between hairy thorns.
In summertime, it was quiet and cool.
Bay laurel trees arched above our heads,
a processional to the graveyard

where golf balls
from the driving range at Trestle Glen
lay buried at the edge of the stream
like giant roe waiting to be fertilized,

some orange, many white, a few
had already shed their outer peel.
They were not our keepers.
Something else had found them.

The game was about how many balls
children could stuff inside their pockets
without rolling back down.
Not the kids. The balls

swelled our pockets, lumps
which were less like grapes
and more like lymph nodes
nursed by loving hands.

And now as I look up the canyon,
past the tangled blackberries
and water spilling over rocks
with pyramids of dog shit

edging the path in mold, all I have left
are hard bits of memory
that line my own pocket.
I touch them over and over again.

Eliza Shefler

Once Again, a Dad by Any Other Name

Dear Daddy, I'm always writing a letter to you
That I never send
Dear Paw-Paw, a tropical fruit
Paws pad-padding around familiarly
In my mind; I was going to read that other poem about you
But couldn't find it in time
I must have inherited your wild
Organizational skills; you'd leave behind a bread-crumb
Paper trail of clues poking out from
Every spare corner, umbilical cords
Linking you to all the alternate realities you could dream up
Dear Poppy, I could never read this poem to you
Were too fragile, a hypnotic, narcotic Oriental
Blossom, friable as tissue, but flaming
Red sun burning against black heart
You bloomed and faded again and again
Folding in on yourself until you disappeared
BDBC, Big Daddy Bear Cat, you called yourself
Pleased, Cheshire Cat smile hanging in the dark
Oscar, bounding warrior, bright spear, O
Scar, spinning in the squirrel cage of your Nordic track
Singing till you drove me crazy
"Would you rather have a mad dad, or a sad dad?"
You spun out gremlins from centrifugal force
The circles slowed; we didn't know until too late
Your heart was turning to stone
Peace, Pappy, a permanent truce has been called
Sing to your heart's content; we'll listen for your voice
Percolating up from underground
Humming in the wind tales of journeys; you passed the test
You don't have to hold up the house of cards anymore
You stared the Gorgon's head
Straight in the eye

Nina Serrano

On Verna's Passing

How can one small word grief *tell it all?*
—Li Qingzhao/Li Ch'ing-chao (1084-1151)

One grief only hints at others
piled high in the charnel house
splintered bones of dusty dreams
hopes hacked asunder by electric saws or lightning bolts
leaving just a hole in the memory
One grief only hints at others
The soul's scrapes and bruises
scabs and calluses
One grief only hints at others

Barbara Joan Tiger Bass

an idea of heaven

glows into the mist
amidst the separate
messes of internal passage
transformed by warmth

lava flows whole toward
this wishful place
this blissful space
outer and inward
wayward and haywire

where meanwhile
the sweet quiet redeems
the chaotic once-in-a-while
while the high-wire risk taker
ascends without fear
and wanders across
mesmerizing heights

as if balance were easy
and the zone of simplicity
could outstretch the raucous
worries of the morass left behind

III

...every thing's a translation of every other thing...

Jeanne Wagner

Puget Sound

A child falls in love
with a name
not knowing it's a place,
only how the first word
clicks shut
neatly as her mother's lacquered box.

Then the second word
opens up,
an angel's oval mouth—shaped-egg
of enunciation.

The vowels begin to sing
for her
their belled sensation.
Sound of the word
sound.

Later she will plumb
its depth,
hear its waves rebound
between
close lying fingers
of land.

Its meaning becoming
clear—now
every thing's a translation
of every other
thing.

Trena Machado

Notes on Writing

Words Over Night

"Almost said." We know what that means. A whole summation of expectation. Things that could be, but not necessarily will. Stopped up in space somewhere, but not now. The pebble in the pond afore, big as the ripples. Not a question of time and distance. Not measurable. No need to measure. Might be metaphor. Hopefully, not. Did we escape?

Polyphonic Mirror

The context/frame(work), produced by intention of the moment, a coin's worth of seeing. More real than the content. You, a you, from a you, no longer what it was, nor what it is.

A Brace of Up & Down

Writing piece in fragments. Or writing long prose. Still wanting one thing to jump to the other, a runner doing hurdles across multiple braces, up, down, flat, up, down, flat and over again. Rhythm. The composition's life. No matter the variation. Listening for the pulse.

Judy Wells

She Liked to Rock the Boat

Louisa May Alcott
        rowed across Walden Pond
                with Thoreau
Oh don't tell me
        he was the one with all the muscle
She was a tomboy
        ran the hills of Concord
                every morning

I can just hear her saying
        to Thoreau "Let me row"
                maybe with a loud "Please"
and then Thoreau would take his
        place in the stern
                and Louisa sat at the oars

Years later she cringed
        when her pre-adolescent girl fans
                besieged her with letters
begging her to make Little Woman Jo
                marry Laurie—
        No, she didn't want to do it—

Why should her alter ego Jo have to marry
        She had rowed Thoreau
                And he didn't marry

Louisa May Alcott refused her public
        and married Jo off to an older professor
                rather than to a romantic youth
I remember my own disappointment
        when I read *Little Men*

but then, at ten, I didn't know
        Louisa had rowed Thoreau
                across Walden Pond

Cherise Wyneken

Re-borne

If I should come around again
I'd choose to come as wind

playful wind

dancing longjohned legs
   clotheslined
hats off
skirts up

sharp wind

coloring stark farmhouse cheeks
   with blotches of red rouge
sifting sand, hedged behind wall studs
creaking windmill arms

wistful wind

strumming mystic music
through fields of whispering wheat
tumbling swelling rests
reaching...rising...

Grace Marie Grafton

Seasonal

after Edouard Vuillard's painting, *The Piano*

There's music today, and wallpaper and rugs,
what used to be called "oriental" patterns.
The women embroider scarves in seasonal
colors, to piano notes. They don't have to think
of anything. Not the arbor where the mistress
was murdered, not the milk gone sour from
keeping too long, not unwanted pregnancies
nor broken fingernails nor lost children.
They are grown up now, none here under sixteen,
they're protected by floral abundance and
batches of Bach. Nothing need tamper with their
focus. Roses smell like vanilla. They admire
each other's cheeks and fingers, the needles slip
noiselessly through the silk. Weather makes
an equation with Best Wishes. These are the days
with no expectations. Peaches loiter on branches.
Later the women will remove their shoes, climb
the ladders and pick the fruit into baskets,
careful not to let fuzz from the peach skins
settle, itchy, into the crooks of their elbows.

Antoinette Constable

Restoration

for Paula Massengill

What are the two women doing
in this painting of a small room? What is
that length of fabric they're bending over?
A patchwork quilt, so worn it isn't worth
mending? What is it they exchange?

You examine the work's margins. The words
"margin of error" come to mind, and you debate
whether, under the yellowed lacquer, the needlework
between the two women could possibly be as old,
say, as the Bayeux Tapestry, with its knights
on horseback, scenes of battles with
blood spurting from falling men, while invisible
women wail beyond the pennants and the tents.

As the solvent works on layers of cracked paint,
an inner courtyard with Doric columns, vines
and three pomegranates start to emerge.
And you finally understand that there,
in front of you, stands Penelope weaving, Penelope
constantly doing and undoing, in order to restore her
self. And you see now that there are two
Penelopes. One on each side of the loom,
matching color strands, admitting patterns,
adjusting tension, replacing knotted
fibers. And you know that the object
passing back and forth between them
is the shuttle of their conversation.

Susan Cohen

Cargador de Flores, Diego Rivera, 1935

It's him! In peasant whites and on all fours, pinned
under the weight of his towering wicker basket.
He stares at the floor of the museum like a mule,

this man who overlooked my childhood from a print
above my parents' bed. He's still burdened by blossoms
piled so high they shove his sombrero down over his brows.

As a girl, I admired the woman: how she leans
to adjust the basket that's fixed
to her man's back by a yellow sling.

Rivera draws my eye from the folds of the sling
to the folds in the woman's cream-colored shawl,
then upward to her lowered eyes.

My mother must have read love here
in all its colors, while my father saw
a laboring man knocked to his knees.

I can hear my father humming Spanish Civil War songs,
union hymns, choruses from battles
he would never risk his family to fight.

I can see my mother tugging up their bedspread,
securing its perfect daily crease with pillows,
as the painting keeps retelling old stories

about the loads of love: of a man
who will never unshoulder his basket, of a woman
who will always be bending to help.

Of a wife who cannot keep herself from worrying
each knot tighter, a husband who wonders
how flowers turned heavy as stones.

Grace Marie Grafton

Fifty-Cent Moon

after Joan Miro's *The Red Sun*

The fifty-cent moon exhilarates the night walkers,
who are foolishly searching for color.
Will silver do? No, longing impels them
to pursue the minute hand into the hours.
Before dawn, the rooster's tail begins
to exalt the rusty eminence it has been
given to crow about. Glory be! The walkers' soles
are sore, their backs near collapse, they
prostrate themselves on rocks and let light swirl
a rainbow around them. These foolish pilgrims
have found their religion. They vow to become
the Johnny Appleseeds of floral largesse. Along
highways, in trashy vacant lots, down wild
watersheds, in parks where state budgets
can no longer pay for weeding, they strew seed
and bury bulbs—poppies, larkspur, Indian paintbrush,
mariposa tulips, Douglas iris, wild pea.
At regular intervals, they deviously return
with their three-wheeled water tank, insuring
the seeds are fed. The water hose sprays
drops that marry sunrays to produce the prism.
Pilgrims' reward.

Evelyn Posamentier

Genetics

i'm contending with the girl in the photo.
it could've been the day she began menstruating.

brain aflutter with lesions, i watch a blood bubble
blossom from the injection site on my thigh.

in the photo the girl knows she will continually
evade adverse events with minimal success.

who goes there, flirting with disability?
in some dreams, there's nothing on the shelves.

at the injection site, curious spirits gather.
the girl in the photo, the lesions, all in collusion.

Christina Hutchins

The Swimmer

Underwater I become a girl
with a young man's ripe back
the muscles curled
around definite bones

But what you saw from above—
a blue-green daemon fraught with ripple
none of my lines a line—   I was broken
shuffled   yet I moved whole

It is me again   at the far side
surfacing   my face and shoulders
reassembled   solidity of my arms established
the settled years refunded

though where I stand waist-deep in the shallows
my hips   my thighs and feet   approximate
one of Picasso's disarticulated women—
I cannot keep my unshackled forms still

IV

...knowing there must be somewhere to go...

Evelyn Posamentier

Attack

i am driving my car through the city.
there are teeth in my brain
beginning to bite at my skin.
i am driving my car through the city
reminding myself to turn my head
before changing lanes.
the radio's on.
thank god for a.m. radio
& all the stupid music
that fights off those teeth.
i keep driving
knowing there must be somewhere to go.
foot on gas pedal.
foot on brakes.
my eyes are familiar with traffic lights.
thank god for that.
if it wasn't for the radio
i'd have to talk to myself.
faster than those teeth.
faster than the gas pedal.
it's gone down to the floor
& the traffic lights begin to blink uncontrollably
& there are more lanes to switch into
& i'm on the freeway now
where no speed limit can stop the car.
only the police.
only the cracked glass & chrome of collision
with my body not talking to itself, but relaxed in separation.
& then i'll have become a surgeon
pulling apart the bodies in my head
separating them from those teeth.
& together with the policeman
i'll have to inform the loved ones
about what happened.

Marianne Betterly

I want to dance

I want to dance like Ginger
swirling with Fred
as if our feet are stitched together,
twirling madly across the white gazebo,
safe from a sudden downpour
but not from each other.

I want to dance like Fred,
buffed black shoes tapping lullabies on cigarette sand
erasing midnight banter
with sprinkles of happily ever after.

I want to dance like Cyd,
whose long legs wrap tight as a Japanese gift box,
spring open, twirl, then
entwine men in a boa embrace.

I want to dance like Michael
zombie jerking, moonwalking across Hollywood,
spinning for Billie Jean and every kid in high tops—
balancing en pointe in tennis shoes,
smiling through the flames.

I want to dance like Gene
splashing in puddles,
tapping black umbrella,
air shoes leaping on lampposts,
heels clicking in wet song.

I want to dance like the Jets
kickbox ballet across empty basketball courts,
finger snapping through graffiti alleys on the West Side,
up wire fences, swimming in heavy air,
floating down the other side,
silently slinking into the shadows
between love and death.

Mary Grover

Crush

She's Ally Sheedy in *High Art*—
not the heroin addict part,
but slouchy-taut and
steaming through faults
where anger has shoved love
under the skin.

As advertised in comic books,
she's sea monkeys,
not the mayonnaise jar
and tap water, brine
shrimp letdown; no, the long-
limbed family, with its democratic
ease of sprouting crowns,
living and breathing
patented pink
impossible.

She's the stomach flu on your birthday,
when you can only watch
Gramma Fritzi remove her ring
to plunge blue-veined hands
into the yolky ooze of ground pork
and beef, bread crumbs soaked in milk,
deftly roll and palm the balls,
make the music of crackle and crisp;
now, gently fold sour cream into the gravy
speckled bright orange—*paprika!*
and there must be green peas and rolls
and butter and cranberry sauce from a can and the moat
of mashed potatoes you would otherwise make.

She's the nautilus,
not the paper devil-
fish, nor the pearly ship,
but canonized in divers' lights,
tentacles streaming from prehistory, clutching
for a mate on TV's undersea world.

A tattoo
fleeting from view,
Isis-kissed ankle.

One pitch shy
of striking out
the Bambino's curse.

She's a thunder egg
laid deep in volcanic soil.

She's the Great Depression,
how it made Mama's ten-cent
ice-cream what it meant
back then.

She's the big bang—
not suns shunning the wink
of their fellows, loping away
to stun the dark of hungry
places, nor barreling back together
to blind the stellar ache; no,

                    my young mother
in a picture, her eyes
the kind of pretty that leaves me
to travel, straddle
a red scooter and pose
for the picture taker,
my distant rival.

Ellaraine Lockie

Translation of a Face-Lift

Words written but unspoken
radiate from the scalpel's thin assault
in colors that bled under her skin
Their sharp blotches a whore's rouge
slap on the face, a fever
fire-engine siren and salmon flesh

The frown she found
in her fourth grade diary
pulled flat now to forge
a platform to speak its mind
A thunderstorm in the swelling
On skin stretched tight like leather
tanned in cedar wood solution

Stains of night, seaweed
saffron, purple plums and dirty linen slurred
Their utterances echoing for days
A sadness that diminishes in hues
of daffodil, dusk, lullaby
pink lemonade and robin's egg

The surgeon said he'd never seen
so much bruising
He hadn't felt the fifty years of silence
secreted behind the frown lines
Nor studied the foreign language of colors
to know how pain can be spelled out
Crayoned powerless by shades of sunshine
How those colors he didn't hear can heal scars

Eva Schlesinger

Napkin Kin

She carries a napkin collection stolen from cafes across America. Napkins are her souvenirs, not postcards, not silver charms, trinkets, or doodads. She has a napkin from a Pennsylvania Dutch pretzel factory, one from the Bronx Zoo, the aquarium, and several she airlifted from the Lebanese restaurant in Mystic. At the grinder store on Bank Street, she plucked napkins from the dispenser while her brother texted his wife on his BlackBerry. Every so often, he'd look up and say, "Stop." In between stops, he'd say, "I do this, too. The napkin stealing."

He told her he had hundreds. She didn't believe him. Months later when he spilled coffee all over his keyboard at work, he popped open the gold snaps to his leather briefcase and retrieved his napkins. First, he snapped a photo with his BlackBerry and sent her an email so she could see for herself.

He was always the best—the first-born, straight-A student, award-winning journalist, and now he held the title for most napkins stolen.

She traveled to Alaska with her supply of napkins. They had been at the bottom of her green batik shoulder bag, but she crammed them in her maroon handbag's outside pocket. Some spilled over the top, peeking out. They had a room with a view, a free ride on a boat, plane, train, and the chance to see wildlife up close.

His napkins stayed stuffed in a briefcase.

They were claustrophobic.

He was, too.

Judith S. Offer

Where Plums Once Hung

I buried my words the other day,
Under the plum, out of the sun,
In the farthest part of the yard.

It was a little hard, parting with
Armloads of my heart's charges:
Unsold poems, unknown stories,

Leftover notes and old programs.
But, I sowed 'em, then hosed 'em over.
It was, surely, a bit absurd.

But it was other words' turns.
These versions had been heard.
They messed my desk, shelf-wrestled,

And pressed endlessly for attention.
It was necessary to eject 'em.
They grumbled some, under the plum,

But I mulched their mumbling.
Now I wonder: will summer sun
Show clumps of puns where plums once hung?

And will my prose turn purpler
Because the plum-under earth's now wordier?

Judy Juanita

Bling!

somebody jumped off slave ships
          fr this
somebody mailed himself in a box
from slavery to freedom
          fr it
somebody else ran like hell
from the paddy rollers
          fr it
& somebody stood up to the koo klux
          fr it
somebody rioted fr it
somebody sang her heart out fr it
somebody blew somebody's socks off fr it
somebody blew his own brains out fr it
somebody died fr yr bling

even as julian bond wrote
look at that girl shake her thing
we can't all be martin luther king
somebody fought just & unjust war
          fr it
somebody died on parchman farm
at the whipping boss' hand
          fr it
somebody became baraka ntozake
madhubuti sekou touré so you cd be
P, snoop, biggie, lil jon, lil kim,
lil slim, jeezy, uncle kracker
somebody else with perfectly decent anglo-
saxon name—fred hampton and mark clark—
died shot to death at four am fr this thing
somebody upheld our long tradition of thought:

dudley randall wrote about the melting pot,
Shove your old pot. You can like it or not,
I'll be just what I am.

somebody died not to be called boy
their noble deaths allow you to be "big boi"
somebody bled to learn the alphabet a to z
giving you license with all 26 letters
& the apostrophe

somebody dreamed not this dream
but a way out of nightmare
& you wake in the middle of it—bling!
thinking it's free and clear but things
aren't always what they seem
somebody died a ludicrous death for ludacris to appear
a son of emmett and ishmael recklessly
eyeballing everyone under the sun

somebody learned the dictionary from aardvark to the end
fr it
somebody's black titties suckled whomever they had to
fr this thing
somebody played maidbutlerdummymammyconvictslave
so you cd be marilyn monroe in blackface
so you cd bring hollywood to the hood

bling

somebody gave one insignificant, unsung, whole wondrous
life fr it

Mary Rudge

This News

Are words terrible enough,
strong enough to tell this—
women in a factory on fire, who burned,
or jumped from windows to fall 9 stories and die—
the poet worked, though words
seemed as blood clots, as tears,
among things that were beautiful in the room,
paintings, photographs, other art and poems,
the heads and hands of people—words fell
from her mind as the women fell, screaming,
the women who sewed the same pattern,
over and over 10 hours a day 7 days a week
12 cents an hour, whose safety was counted
as nothing—146 died, their bodies were counted—
even after a hundred years, they haunt in news—
the burning skin of live bodies on fire,
sizzle of fat, flesh, the ache in hands that
could not hold longer to the edge of a window,
the agony of fear in the falling,
the instant white light of blank emptiness
when the brain spills from the skull's crack,
the breaking of spine and fingers,
the intertangled neural system,
blood vessels, sinew, split open, girls and
women who were once solid forms
in a room humming with their industry,
warm with their breath, with feelings
and neurons throbbing and tingling—
women who shared bread they needed
with others in need, the girl with beads
and ribbons braided into her hair,
the woman who sang songs she knew

from another place to her children, the one
others counted on for their happiness, who
made things beautiful—for these, the poet
tried to gather together words and letters that
were scattered like separate bones—for women
who had sold parts of their lives for passage to
America—women with years of sweat and tears
in the thousands of stitches they made for so
few coins—the one who was 13 years old—
women who had come from persecution and
repression, to here and hope—those who
hung from window sills by their fingertips—
girls who gave their virginity to get a job—
women who slept on cardboard—women with
7 children 12 children—the one who supported
a sick mother and little sisters—the one who died
with the unborn child within her—the ones who
held hands and fell through space together—
the one who kissed her and pushed her out the
window 9 stories up, then jumped, hair on fire,
through the air—the many who fell into the
firemen's nets then onto the sidewalk as others
fell upon them and the nets broke, their fall
broke through concrete—they burned and
outrage changed things, fire sprinklers spring out
overhead like lotus, opening—
they died for unlocked doors and safe elevators
and fire escapes, for unions and working conditions
to become humane—the artist wants to show
fair labor laws, workers' rights, justice—the poet
tries again to shape words into action and truth—
artists and poets together, what will our work do—
and you, too, what more can we do with this news?

Andrena Zawinski

Turning a Train of Thought Upside Down
(or What We Learn)

...as a woman, I have no country. As a woman I want no country.
As a woman, my country is the whole world... —Virginia Woolf

Under the bottlebrush tree the lovers sit,
circled by each other's arms, all alone
right in front of us all
on our walks around the city lake,
their kisses blind to the afternoon
breathing down on them and us.

I think of my own first love,
how a woman can learn not to take
but to give, how not to gain a self
but to lose one inside another—
natural as breathing, to be in exile
under her own skin, colonized
without knowing she was occupied.

Long ago, women in my family
carried bundles of wash on their backs
down to the creek bed to scrub it all clean,
later balanced books on their heads
for good posture and the possibility
of a cover shot on a fashion magazine,
having been fed a diet of Cinderella,
Sleeping Beauty, the Snow White tales.

Just look at the statistics—how many
of us have sported the split lips,
bruised eyes, broken limbs,
how many assaulted and betrayed,
how many isolated and afraid,

our homes gone up in flames
from so many hearts afire.

Yet we have resisted and rebelled,
conquered enemies, negotiated peace.
We have also had our feet bound,
bodies girdled and gagged, some buried
beneath layers of cloth. We have been
overthrown, dispossessed, imprisoned,
enslaved, burned wholesale at the stake.

We have also been venerated and feared
as Congolese leading warriors into battle
with shields and spears, as Mongolians
riding steeds armed with bows and arrows,
as Seneca ruling the land and the clan
drumming and healing, as Balkans singing
in the company of women just for the song.

Some of us now build muscles in our legs
and take to running for the thrill of the race,
work them in our arms wielding swords
and wrestling whatever might confront us.
We grow strong enough to carry ourselves
to our own shade tree, dream beneath its leaves
in the kiss of our own breath, learn to love
ourselves deeply and with great abandon.

V

...we are beginning to understand something...

Gail Rudd Entrekin

Something Coming

We are beginning to understand something
of what is coming, to go beyond sensing a shadow
in the woods watching us, and to see it take shape,
see it coming toward us across a field, zigzagging
as it does, now standing idle and watching the sky,
now heading directly for us at a trot. And realizing
that we are seen, that it will find us no matter
what we do, we are slowing down.
                                        We are
standing very still hoping to blend with the waving
greens of this raw springtime, to stay downwind
of it as warmer breezes pick up and buffet the leaves,
the grasses, tossing everything in a moving salad
of life; we sway on our legs, trying to move with the air
that surrounds us, and we stop thinking of what is around
the next bend in the path, stop planning our next
escape route, and begin to merge with the moment;
we have slipped into a painting by van Gogh;
something is coming again across the fields and we
are open as sunflowers in full bloom
to these last moments on the earth.

Patti Trimble

Below Isberg Pass

Each summer I imagine myself a voyager
to the unknown, my high meadow wilderness
some beloved green sea, my heart
a gyroscope that spins to the high view
where river runs to cloud.

I must go there in those brief and fragile months.
I must memorize flowers that hang from threads,
columbine, cinquefoil, or the tiniest white daisies.

But where I once thought the sky trembled
the boulder shivered for every god in need of a home,
I now believe it shakes in fear of me
and see behind me deepening trenches
across this Earth I meant to love.

Judy Bebelaar

Red-Tailed Hawk

In spring's green ease
a pair of red-tailed hawks
draws slow easy circles
high above a windy field.
The male begins to plummet
and rise, over and over,
his wings miracles of arch and reach,
his eyes, cut obsidian, yellow fire.
He touches her, and then the two,
pulling light through widespread feathers,
grasp talons and spiral down,
a wild courtship
against brilliant coastal blue.

From the shambles of summer
they fashion a nest
woven of wildness,
rustle of wind in grass,
steady beat of sea on rock,
bark and husks and stalks.

Autumn, her chicks, soft and wary,
watch from high in a tall eucalyptus
as the female circles over the field,
hovers, then slips down,
a flash of darkness trailing light.
Her mate, nearby,
follows her sweep
to the grass.

Christina Hutchins

Into your pocket

I have slid a bright morning before rain.
Tonight's concerto is folded into thousands
of paper cranes; their wings were trees, rollicking
restless in the sun. Here's a loose,
black thread pulled from my hem, tangled

to a tiny bundle between my fingers & thumb.
Kelp strands roiled back & forth in the surf
& deposited at high tide, the lost chains
of underseas are knotted, left along the beach.
Here is the warmth of my stride, left in a heap

on a rug beside the bed, blue jeans shed
in the shapes of my legs. I, too, have held
the shape of an absence. Quiet in the auditorium.
Who is that, laughing at the back of the room?
Here we are again, leaning against the door,

my way to you disclosed by two tongues
spending a sweet moment. The self I become
& the self you become are celestial bodies
entered into, one by another. Tender
release, a wet palate tasting its small

flourishes, my love is for taking along.
Like you, I swim a rising, astral surge.
If we are anchored by every spent moment,
the anchors are already rusted to dust
& these chains no heavier than light.

Antoinette Constable

Trail at Muir Woods

The past is held inside hundreds of concentric layers
of wood in shades of smoke, eggshell, and faded
cinnamon. The official markers give us mostly
public causes for rejoicing: the granting
of the Magna Carta, the Crusades,
Napoleon's final exile to the Isle of Elba,
the signing of the Declaration of Independence.
I plant private markers for the first time I knotted
loops to tie my shoes, the first time I sprouted
beans in cotton wool; also for finding out
what had defeated my gifted emperor-father who
drew surely better than Michelangelo when
Tuberculosis forced him into exile. He died
in a sanatorium in Switzerland. For him I plant

forget-me-nots. I wear his watch as marker
for the day his triple coffin was set down
dead in the middle of our bare living room, a gift from
our grandfather, wrathful god whose spirit could not
accept his loss. This last grand and parental gesture
toward his dead son cost more than
what the four of us lived on for two war years. Then
I wrote the declaration of my independence choosing
to leave when I finished high school, marking the day
by setting free a ladybug caught on a drape with a flick
of an index finger over my thumb. I live now

in California where new leaves have grown
on my family tree fed by recent roots in the loam
sending the sequoia forever skyward, fire-safe
in live bark, that skin between sapwood and outside
world, in an ever expanding layer between past and future.
The path, lined with ferns edged in water drops,
charms me like an invitation. A salmon swims upstream.

Judy Wells

By Walden Pond

I was sitting by Walden Pond
        looking at the water
It was raining so the water was stirred up

I saw a man emerging from the water
It was Thoreau himself, hatless
        in dark jacket and pants
holding forth his hand
        and contemplating it

He looked deeply into its palm
        and did not seem to notice me at all
so absorbed was he in studying
        his own miracle

Then he began to sink back down
        into the water
I watched him go—black pants
        black suit jacket, then his face
                and dark locks
till only his hand stretched
        over his head

It suddenly reached out and touched mine
My hand opened the way his did
        and then he disappeared

I stood there by the pond
        now contemplating my hand
wondering what mystery
        an open hand
                contained

Manja Argue

The Wind

In the high desert
of northern Nevada,
the wind arises.
Without warning
it scrapes unimpeded
across the landscape.
Lonely aspen trees
dance with the wind
that tugs at them,
inviting them
to abandon their roots.

I love the sound,
the smell, the feel
of the wind.
I wonder does it know me
when it wraps its
arms around me
tugging at my sleeve.
I hear it now
in the music of the leaves
singing a song of passion
calling for my surrender.

Cherise Wyneken

Viewed from the Alhambra

Are we really all so different—you and I?
You who quartered women in seraglios
niched near tiled pools,
Moorish caliph, come to capture Spain.

I can understand your
love of beauty—poets' words
engraved within your walls,
keyhole windows
peeking on vast views,
fountains, spewing from a lion's lips,
holy cleansing pools.
Clay stalactites, tapering into blue,
caved corridor of pillared arches
laid with Mother of Pearl,
filigreed, open into court.

I can understand your
strong desire—retiring to the garden
beyond protective moats,
walking midst the molded Cyprus
past dark ponds where lilies float.

Oh, King, residing in Alhambra,
my garden's small compared to yours,
my palace plain and dull,
and yet I, too, find peace
behind their simple walls.

Gloria Rodriguez

Afternoon Sounds

I sat
sipped iced root beer
listened to afternoon sounds
in day's last glare

Leaves fell
from summer's heat
they seemed to huddle and wait
for day's cool end

Bees came to settle
only stragglers buzzed by
confused as to direction
they ignored my *tapas*

Lizards scurried in and out of brambles
wondered
I'm sure
why I sat in the shade and just munched

Then the sun
sank below the horizon
everything was left aglow
in translucent colors

Soon the sky dimmed
preparing for evening's wonder
patiently I sat
waiting for new sounds to begin

Zara Raab

Hogback

The blue Chevy with the windows down
is his idea of indoors, summers;
he has the cast of mind of hogback,
the temperament of coarse-grained basalt;
his stained, half-missing fingers fisted
over the wheel, he cusses, and pulls
the trigger on a harem of does,
(and misses) downwind in the tare grass,
then roars into third so's to bypass
thinning pinewoods and ferret the coves
for three braces of pearly mollusk.
He's a jack-of-all-trades. Come sundown
to the lit sawmill, he'll strut around,
trimming the burl and burning the husks.

His new woman stands by the oven
of her gold-dun kitchen, baking rusks,
she has a mind of wide open fields,
at home in fescue, tare and chickweed.
Come Sundays, he jaws the venison,
she revs the Chevy's V-8 engine,
or sights along a twenty-two:
She's coming along, he says, none too soon.
This very morning she took her knapsack
to the blue-lupin pastures, loony
as a bluebird among the dobbins.
Any day now, she'll mount the hogback,
track bucks with points on the knobby spine,
and shoot to kill, too, and not soften.

Carol Dorf

Plotting Hours of Daylight

Already there's a perceptible change of light and darkness, the rush of time that speeds up around the equinox—and no one feels quite ready for the change. That's how we always imagine infinite, as though we believe the proof that maps all the real numbers into the space between zero and one. She holds out her hand, and we expect a gift, but instead it is a small frog, the toxic slime about its skin shiny in this light. How did she become immune? One smiles, as running is not an option and then a bell rings and it's time to go to class; we are all in that infinite high school where every moment presages disaster, and we always want to tell more to our friends than will ever be safe. Between light and dark, twilight, which always used to frighten me because the approach of night was more of a problem than darkness itself. When I switch off the light, shadows lengthen and lose form, the way the lost are everywhere filling the corners of the room, calling out: "Look at me, stop that purposeful forgetting." There's pressure to rejoice in winter as though crystals encompass perfection. I used to fear the melt. Where were you then? The way we walked hand in hand, spooned together through night, like the infinite colors of another country.

Gloria Rodriguez

Upside Down Again

When I was a young girl
standing on my head and hands
from time to time was fun

Recently I felt like doing it again
but at my age the approach
had to be a bit different

Bending down at waist height until
my hands supported me on ground
then turning my head
so everything was upside down
my eyes gazed upon a
common picture from a different and
painful point of view

Blue was at the bottom
golden foothills on top and
strokes of gnarled geometry
with splotches of green
painted in the middle

Upside down certainly gave me a
different perspective and
appreciation of how I was
to get right side up again

Tobey Kaplan

Calling out the end of shadows

singing within the earth
I wander around a darkened house where the heart echoes
those wonderful questions inside no one knows
calling dogs and cats
blending into an ocean of air
not too long from night's
shifting reason and meaning
and what it is to be wrong

I get home before dinner
then walk dogs at midnight
not too long we complain fast
the way breathing and too long always
gets left alone with whatever you make me feel like

we are far from each other
calling out
across the telling

Trena Machado

Winter

A calling to go down to the hard point, for the strength of things.
The timber's core, power in the wave, how empty the sky can
be and still be there. The call shifting within to match the fire
held in things. A fire, not revealed upon the asking, not given
up as a thing that can be seen. Timber facing what comes,
over and over the wave breaks, the sky everywhere steadfast.
That which continues.

VI

...I see the purpose of everything around me...

Ellaraine Lockie

Saying Good-Bye

The cut daffodils on the kitchen table
turn dark gold after two weeks
Out of the window late afternoon sun
emblazons bark on a madrona tree
to a deep cherry sheen

Such light is a living thing
Like the deer that strip ribbons of red from bark
Or woodpeckers that eat the orange
puckered berries
Such light never shone inside a church
Not in sixty years of Sundays

A searchlight for lost souls
For the downtrodden, the sick, the guilty, the sad
The hearts beaten into a flat line
It sucks me to its bosom
Elevates me to high branches
where I see the purpose
of everything around me

The bee in the wild rose bush
Why the waves in the ocean
The robin's song at dusk
The onset of night
The circular motion of the stars

It is here in this tree where I leave you
My wings as butterfly brittle as a dead daffodil
Before it crumbles into the earth
to become bone meal for the roots

Eva Schlesinger

Steering Your Walker

I see you gliding there along the high-toned hospital floor.
—Carol Tufts

I see you gliding there along the high-toned hospital floor
as though it's your highway
steering your walker,
a nurse to your right,
her hand steadying you
You are thirty-two going on thirty-three
You had plans to spend this summer biking,
but are learning to walk again instead
Your face shines red
an outspoken burn
You stagger and lurch
like Frankenstein's monster
You pause
To
Catch
Your
Breath

Patti Trimble

In the Women's Hammam, Kairouan

I wanted to be a mute creature, the most common miracle
to the women who rubbed their hands up my thighs
and slapped the sponge against my buttocks

just because they towed me to some watery shore
I'd never seen before and tried to lose me in a fog
that glowed white upon luminous white, just because

I glimpsed the limbs of giants swimming coral undersea
and two brown arms poured what looked like clarity

as they lifted my hooves, scraped down my shanks,
lathered my neck and mane, whacked me gently with a towel—

And because three young girls stared at me.

If not animal, well-worn rug, loaf of bread

Marianne Betterly

Recycling

They are late today
screeching brakes outside my house
then a staccato of backup beeps,
cans rolling,
and the grinding, mashing
as all our leftovers are taken away.

Tucked between the morning paper and empty envelopes—
a few of your unsent letters in
distinctive pen and dipped blue ink,
the curves of your Y and R
become smiling eyes
across the breakfast table while
writing a card to a monk in Kathmandu
between sips of espresso and cinnamon toast.

Your words now trucked
to a paper afterlife,
maybe compacted into a cube
or mixed with coffee grounds and egg shells.

I didn't toss them all,
made just enough space
for a few new cards in a different hand mingled with
photos of evening star cymbidiums,
Paris at dusk,
the cartwheel galaxy floating like jellyfish,
and a wish or two.

Janell Moon

Triptych of Membrane

I.
Identity follows me around like a dog thrashing about after a swim.
I've never had a dog or been on a farm, not sure I'd care to stimulate
another tomato. I'm a-this-and-a-that, and in the flash of film,
a cigarette tumbles out of the pack of my mind. *No smoking in*
the dark, the sign says. Weird, hadn't smoked for years but now
the craving. Cigarettes, chemicals, commas, and coma, the edge
of the flesh appears as the dog and I disappear, reappear into
birth's mottled breath.

II.
I bang my head on the roof of the world again and again, but there's
no sound. How to write a body swollen as sadness. Undocumented
flesh. The edge of the blue blanket, satin breast, wash of the mother
body pasted together—imagination and insistence. No need for strings,
the mask is thin, and there is no bruise that does not remember its own
bruising.

III.
A tendency of the family for head-on crashes creates a shift to the
other side of fate. Here we are holding our own small baggage of coins
to buy weddings and teeth and we crash down into a ravine with its
run of skunks. My sister holds tightly to the lace edge of her dress
stored in a Safeway sack, the plastic flapping its mirror. Ohio, humidity,
our blood stolen by mosquitoes. She tells us to sit on our hands and we
obey. This is her day gone badly. Suddenly I slide down the hill to join
them saying, *I can talk pigeon. I speak a little bird.*

Jan Steckel

Wake

No funeral, he said, just a roaring party,
so she threw out the medical gizmos,
stacked canvasses to the ceiling
to clear up floor space, stored up ice.
She painted from photographs of him
when he was still well, five, ten,
fifteen years ago, to drive out
his last days gasping in the hospital.
In the paintings, his beard was full,
still part brown. His smile invited you in.
She hung them on the bedroom walls
to keep her company while she slept,
moved them to the living room for the party.

Friends drove up from San Diego,
down from the Oregon border,
in from their suburban diaspora.
They brought turkey, hazelnut cake,
diabetes, breakups that wouldn't stay broken,
hepatitis C, beer, dope, Two-Buck Chuck,
bad backs, bum knees, drug convictions,
half-bottles of port and whiskey,
smoker's hacks, monkeys on their backs.
They played banjo, accordion,
guitar and mandolin. Irish reels,
Bob Dylan songs, with radio
tuned to saxophone in the bedroom.
Stories of the dead man rose, consolidated
in the smoky air, winked, bowed,
joined hands, and danced in slow roundelays.

She carried his boxed ashes
through the crowded room.
He weighed so much.
She had to set him down,
sink onto the couch.
She looked up at the walls.
From one painting to the next,
his cheeks grew fuller,
his skin rosier, his lips redder,
his eyes happier. He got younger
stronger, more himself, till the wizened,
bald, yellow-skinned invalid in the ICU
faded like an ancient Polaroid.

Eliza Shefler

Dust Chanty

It sifts down from the sky
Draping in slow   even   measures
Every unprotected surface
Wipe the windowsill with your hand
It always feels the same, grey
Chalky as your grandmother's powder
The faint, peppery choking:
        Atoms surrendering to time
        Steadily grind into softness
        Even the skin you shed
        Incessantly shreds itself into
Dust
        Thick wax encasing old books
Dust
        Greasy film of years you can't scrub clean
Dust
        Kissing your fingertip
        As you write your name on the mirror
Dust
        Your enemy, dulling everything
        Smothering the air as it falls relentlessly
        On the floor you just vacuumed
        Again
Dust
        Your friend
        Coating the world with itself
        So you won't forget the bond
        Of air   to rock   to plant   to flesh   to
Dust

Eileen Malone

This Gold Is Horseflesh

Flying yet floating, a crest of grazing horses
rises from between rounded hill breasts
not a crash of sunset, more a metallurgical glow
of horse-herd caught suspended in late sun fire

so, this is it, the Eldorado of which they speak
everywhere, everywhere, gold poured on gold
illuminated, anointed, like legend, but unlike
for this gold is horseflesh, burnished beasts

then a dark cloud, at once, the sun retreats
my own mare prances in place, in shadow
Eldorado dissipates; fog curls up from the sea
we reestablish ourselves as rider and ridden

complete the circle around the riderless herd
that returns to common dun, bay, yellowed white
retired horses, swayback, shedding, put out to pasture
nuzzling white doe droppings on dry, dead grass

quickly laminating gold dusted photographs
stuck between the cellophane of my eyes
we trot back to the barn, never once turning back
before all the glory dies out entirely.

Nina Serrano

The Past

Sometimes the past slams the door in your face
Even if you phone first to say that you are coming
Even if you politely bring
a bouquet of flowers and a box of candy
It's no matter to the impervious past
that doesn't care about future consequences
because they already happened.
The past turns its back and leaves me
pounding on its portals.
My cries echo in the dust.

Tobey Kaplan

the luxury of the past

roadsters riding the toll road through Alley Park
write about horses in the stable
and what sprung up around trees
asphalt and gravel through the mud slopes
the Long Island Motor Parkway all torn up
passing by the Dix Hills home of Coltrane's sax
where the revamped roads and overpasses remain
in the Queens neighborhood where I shuffled
overgrown pathways hands in worn coats torn pockets
sweat and music layers under the road and knobby roots
bursting out from concrete spectrum of rusty light
bleached around foggy mist a teaspoon in the dirt
a pair of goggles and cracked gloves
the Long Island of Whitman's trust in his leaves
and grass the perception of longing and innocence
that knotted and tangled history what can only inspire
as old poet Walt rode the ferry from Brooklyn
imagined freeing both slaves and masters

Nanette Deetz

He Ce Tu Ado Mi Taku Oyasin

(Dakota: *Many Blessings to Full Circle of Relatives*)
for Ken James Bradley, Spirit Walk: March 26, 1976

I live on an island now,
surrounded by the sounds of water.
Songbirds,
Red-tailed hawk, blue heron, egret, blue jay and crow.
Here is where I deny urban reality,
this New World.
My relatives taught me early the trick to Indian survival.
How to make the square a circle,
how to make concrete, cars, and pain disappear.
They taught us how to look at our land
and see it as it was 511 years ago.
Ken taught us to remember
the season when choke cherries ripen.
To remember
the stars and the star people.
To remember
the gift of knowledge passed through a good story
and a good joke.
To remember
to sing and dance,
sing and dance.
Mixed race woman
mixed race man,
caught in the gauze between two worlds,
our minds and senses the only means of escape.
But scar tissue lies thick and deep.
Too many broken promises,
broken treaties,
broken hearts.
Loved ones taken away, or leaving us behind,
have made our eyes weak,
but our hearts
sharp and clear.
Deer, wolf, bear, buffalo.

Lynne Knight

The Deer Near El Mirador

Rain smashes waxy petals from the tulip trees,
washes the last of fallen plum blossoms down
the drain where pine needles and other debris
threaten to give way. I start to kick them back
with my boot, yanking the dog from nosing them,

as a deer appears at the top of El Mirador path,
not panting or showing other signs of the steep climb
as a human would, though she seems human
the way she startles and looks about. I call to her.
Good morning, deer! and hear, *Good morning, dear,*

and hear myself a querulous old woman,
greeting her husband at breakfast while cursing
under her breath, life so vast with disappointments
she doesn't know where to start to name them.
But the dog saves me again, barks, barks

until the deer turns, bounds down the steps,
nothing but her black tail visible against the blur
of rain and redwoods. Then nothing but the rain,
the dog and me, the quiet street. We head for
the waterfall, leaving the querulous old woman

behind. Let her be. I'll pretend not to know her
if I see her in the mirror, or disappear her
by remembering the waterfall, the dog
barking joyously as if the water's alive, loud
enough to quiet dread, to outsing everything.

Zara Raab

Whiskey

In the hollows of lightning-struck trees,
deep in the forest of the Weotts,
the fathers ran their stills when you were
still a boy by the cold-running Eel;
they hid the cucurbit of berries,
the mash of scented, fermenting grain,
and lit their secret flames below, then
by every hook and crook jury-rigged
a rick for aging the casks of gin.

Blessed be these makeshift alembics
passed down to you—all else there was oath
and curse, every half breath a "damn it,"
or "hell," so thank God, thank the Scotsman
for the waters of life that cleanse you,
the *usquebaugh*, the bourbon whiskey,
raw as salt searing the quenched throat,
turning to vapor all troubles,
de-fanged an evening and slow-content.

Lucille Lang Day

Returning to The Butchart Gardens

Fifty years ago, rushing ahead of my parents
and friend Sharon, I ran down these same paths
edged with lobelias and blue poppies
on Vancouver Island. Sea hollies bobbed
like small purple pinecones on stalks, canna lilies
waved pink silks, begonias danced in several shades
of red. The Sunken Garden, once a limestone quarry,
overflowed with dahlias and hydrangeas. I'd never
been in an airplane; no one had a cell phone
or computer; no one had walked on the moon.

What have I done these fifty years? Fell in love
with a field of wild irises and a boy I met
at Al's Drive-In when I was fourteen, wore
a tight, blue-satin Chinese dress to our wedding
seven months later, bore a daughter while pink
and lavender mariposa tulips opened, left
my husband, stapled lids to chicken dinner plates
for a living, missing the blue-runner violet's
spectacular display, married the same man
again at seventeen, while slender sunflowers
nodded their yellow heads in an autumn breeze,
left him again in spring, when fire poppies ignited
the coastal range, learned to solve differential
equations and identify the parts of a flower
(pistil, stigma, style, ovary, anther, filament),
fell in love with a man who said at a party,
"You look like you want to dance," married
him in a meadow by a redwood grove
where chickweed looked like drifts of snow,
bore another daughter, measured the electrical

potential across the membrane of an egg cell
of a mud whelk, wrote technical manuals,
left my husband, taught students to distinguish
between monocots and dicots by the veins
in their leaves, interviewed scientists, wrote about
how the universe bloomed from a single seed,
ran a health museum, wrote poems filled
with wildflowers, fell in love again, married
him under a canopy whose poles were twined
with pink, red, white and yellow roses, held
bronze urns containing my parents' ashes
on a hillside above the bay, read *Bambi*, played
Candy Land, and watched *Cinderella* and *Dumbo*
with my grandchildren while seasons changed
and the rhododendrons in my front yard grew
heavy again with bell-shaped flowers.

Of course, Mrs. Butchart's gardens look different
now, smaller, the roses no longer in bloom.
Arched trellises, once laden with red blossoms
hanging over the path, are wound with empty vines.
I reach the end, the Italian Garden—so genteel
with its walkways and cross-shaped central bed
of marigolds and peonies—just before the gift shop.
But I want to go back, so I run to the head
of the path and make a mad dash, sprinting now
back toward the Sunken Garden for one more look
before the delphiniums and begonias fade.

Nellie Hill

Continuum

The watery light calls me
and the drumming of rain
pushes me. The kitchen
ingredients wait to be blended.

As I watch the hillside
reddening with the rising sun
and hours later
reddening with the lowering sun
my mind settles too,
ready for evening
and the changes that come,
that draw me back to the dream,
to the irresistible mystery
of the almost understood.

Judy Bebelaar

Some Birds

All of us try to keep up,
though mostly, we creep.
We are locked in
to our pasts.
We are books
written by authors
whose names we have forgotten,
living as in a dream
until something pushes us
over the edge
or we wake up,
feel the heaviness of autumn,
the chill at the sky's corners.
Already, we notice.
So soon this year, we think.
The leaves have turned.
The squirrels have begun to nibble
at the green persimmons,
and finding them bitter,
throw them down.
Still, some birds sing.
The finches have fledged,
moved on,
so tiny and trim,
so focused on being alive.

Index

Acknowledgments

Some of the poems in this book appeared previously as indicated below. They are reprinted here by permission of the authors.

Manja Argue: "The Wind," *Sundays at the Bugamvilla/Domingos En El Bugamvilla* (Sundays at the Bugamvilla, 2004).

Judy Bebelaar: "Red-Tailed Hawk," *The Crazy Child Scribbler*, 2011.

Ruby Bernstein: "Ritual," *Digital Paper*, 2011.

Susan Cohen: "Chamber Music," *Seattle Review*, 2003; "*Cargador de Flores*, Diego Rivera, 1935," *Southern Poetry Review*, 2010. Both poems also appear in *Throat Singing* (Cherry Grove Collections, 2012).

Carol Dorf: "Fruit of Stories," *Babel Fruit*, 2008; "Plotting Hours of Daylight," *The Prose-Poem Project*, 2010/2011.

Gail Entrekin: "Deciding," *Manorborn* and *Green Hills Literary Lantern*, 2010; "Something Coming," *Nimrod*, 2011, as a finalist for the Pablo Neruda Prize.

Rebecca Foust: "Mom's Canoe," *Atlanta Review*; "Apologies to my OB-GYN," *Margie*. Both poems also appear in *All That Gorgeous Pitiless Song* (Many Mountains Moving Press, 2010).

Christina Hutchins: "Into your pocket," *The Missouri Review*, 2010, as the winner of the Jeffrey E. Smith Editors' Prize; "The Swimmer," *The Cream City Review*, 2005. "The Swimmer" also appears in *The Stranger Dissolves* (Sixteen Rivers Press, 2011).

Bonnie Kwong: "Common Flower," *Families: The Frontline of Pluralism* (Wising Up Press, 2008); "To Unborn Sons," *Yellow as Turmeric, Fragrant as Cloves* (Deep Bowl Press, 2008).

Ellaraine Lockie: "Translation of a Face-Lift," *Mudfish*, 2008; "Saying Good-bye," *Georgetown Review*, 2009.

Trena Machado: "Notes on Writing," *Ambush Review*, 2010.

Eileen Malone: "How She Brushed Her Hair," second prize, Milton Dorfman Poetry competition, 2006; "This Gold is Horseflesh," *The Haven*, 1986.

Dawn McGuire: "True North," *Nimrod*, 2005.

Janell Moon: "Triptych of Membrane," *Ambush Review*.

Judith S. Offer: "And Theirs, Them," *The First Apples* (Shakespeare's Sisters Press, 1977).

Evelyn Posamentier: "Attack," *American Poetry Review*, 1977; "Genetics," *Diagram*, 2004.

Zara Raab: "Whiskey," *Red Lines Blues*, 2011; "Hogback," *The Dark Horse*, 2010. Both poems also appear in *Swimming the Eel* (WordTech Communications, 2011).

Gloria Rodriguez: "Afternoon Sounds," *Yesterdays* (Benicia Library First Tuesdays Poets Anthology, 2007) and *Colored Piece of Froth* (Rock & Feather Publications, Bookworm Press, 2008).

Mary Rudge: "This News" appeared in an exhibit at the Benicia Library, California.

Nina Serrano: "The Past," *Think-Ink.net*, 1999; "On Verna's Passing," *GeoCities.com*, 1995.

Jan Steckel: "Wake," *The Horizontal Poet* (Zeitgeist Press, 2011).

Jeanne Wagner: "My mother was like the bees," *California Quarterly*, 2010. It also appears in *In the Body of Our Lives* (Sixteen Rivers Press, 2010).

Cherise Wyneken: "Viewed from the Alhambra," *Poets Online*, 2000.

Andrena Zawinski: "Turning a Train of Thought Upside Down," *Paterson Literary Review*. It also appears in *Something About* (Blue Light Press, 2009).

About the Editor

Andrena Zawinski's collection of poetry *Something About* (2009, Blue Light Press) is a 2010 recipient of a PEN-Oakland Josephine Miles Award. Her collection *Traveling in Reflected Light* (1995, Pig Iron Press) received a Kenneth Patchen Prize in Poetry. Her poems have appeared in numerous literary publications—including *Many Mountains Moving, Nimrod, Rattle, Slipstream, Quarterly West, Gulf Coast,* and *Progressive Magazine*—and have been widely anthologized.

Her other collections include *Taking the Road Where It Leads* (2008, Poets Corner Press); *Zawinski's Greatest Hits 1991-2001* (2002, Pudding House Publications); *Elegies for My Mother* (1998), an online collection at *The Pittsburgh Quarterly*; *Poems from a Teacher's Desk* (1993, Harris Publications); and *Six-Pack Poems-to-Go* postcard collection (1993, Harris Publications). She has co-edited *Writing on the Desk: Poems and Prose by Teachers of the Western Pennsylvania Writing Project* Celebrating Ten Years at the University of Pittsburgh (1994, WPWP, University of Pittsburgh).

Zawinski has been a longtime feminist and activist in the Women Against Violence Against Women Movement. She founded and organizes the San Francisco Bay Area Women's Poetry Salon. She is also Features Editor at PoetryMagazine.com.

Also from Scarlet Tanager Books

Bone Strings by Anne Coray
poetry, 80 pages, $15.00

Wild One by Lucille Lang Day
poetry, 100 pages, $12.95

The "Fallen Western Star" Wars: A Debate About Literary California, edited by Jack Foley
essays, 88 pages, $14.00

Catching the Bullet & Other Stories by Daniel Hawkes
fiction, 64 pages, $12.95

Luck by Marc Elihu Hofstadter
poetry, 104 pages, $16.00

Visions: Paintings Seen Through the Optic of Poetry
by Marc Elihu Hofstadter
poetry, 72 pages, $16.00

Embrace by Risa Kaparo
poetry, 70 pages, $14.00

crimes of the dreamer by Naomi Ruth Lowinsky
poetry, 82 pages, $16.00

red clay is talking by Naomi Ruth Lowinsky
poetry, 142 pages, $ 14.95

The Number Before Infinity by Zack Rogow
poetry, 72 pages, $16.00

Call Home by Judy Wells
poetry, 92 pages, $15.00

Everything Irish by Judy Wells
poetry, 112 pages, $12.95

CPSIA information can be obtained at www.ICGtesting.com
Printed in the USA
LVOW061021220112
264984LV00001B/6/P

9 780976 867623